I0013673

YOUR KNOWLEDGE HAS \

- We will publish your bachelor's and master's thesis, essays and papers

- Your own eBook and book - sold worldwide in all relevant shops

- Earn money with each sale

Upload your text at www.GRIN.com
and publish for free

Chozha Raja, Ramiah Ilango

Extended Annotating Search Results from Web Databases

GRIN Publishing

Imprint:

Copyright © 2013 GRIN Verlag GmbH
Print and binding: Books on Demand GmbH, Norderstedt Germany
ISBN: 978-3-656-54641-2

This book at GRIN:

http://www.grin.com/en/e-book/265056/extended-annotating-search-results-from-web-databases

GRIN - Your knowledge has value

Since its foundation in 1998, GRIN has specialized in publishing academic texts by students, college teachers and other academics as e-book and printed book. The website www.grin.com is an ideal platform for presenting term papers, final papers, scientific essays, dissertations and specialist books.

Visit us on the internet:

http://www.grin.com/

http://www.facebook.com/grincom

http://www.twitter.com/grin_com

Extended Annotating Search Results from Web Databases

-Chozha Raja P
SBM College of Engineering & Technology,

-Ramiah Ilango
SBM College of Engineering & Technology,

Abstract:
When a query is submitted to a search engine, the search enginereturns a dynamically generated result page containing the resultrecords, each of which usually consists of a link to and/or snippetof a retrieved Web page. In addition, such a result page often alsocontains information irrelevant to the query, such as informationrelated to the hosting site of the search engine and advertisements.In this paper, we present a technique for automatically producingwrappers that can be used to extract search result records fromdynamically generated result pages returned by search engines.As the popular two-dimensional media, the contents on Web pages are always displayed regularly for users to browse.This motivates us to seek a different way for deep Web data extraction to overcome the limitations of previous works by utilizing someinteresting common visual features on the deep Web pages. In this paper, a novel vision-based approach that is Web-pageprogramming-language-independent is proposed. This approach primarily utilizes the visual features on the deep Web pages toimplement deep Web data extraction, including data record extraction and data item extraction. We also propose a new evaluationmeasure revision to capture the amount of human effort needed to produce perfect extraction. Our experiments on a large set of Webdatabases show that the proposed vision-based approach is highly effective for deep Web data extraction.A meta search engine supports unified access to multiplecomponent search engines. To build a very large-scaleMeta search engine that can access up to hundreds ofthousands of component search engines, one majorchallenge is to incorporate large numbers of autonomoussearch engines in a highly effective manner. To solve thisproblem, we propose automatic search engine discovery,automatic search engine connection, and automatic searchengine result extraction techniques. Experiments indicate that these techniques are highly effective and efficient.

1. INTRODUCTION

Search engines are very important tools for people to reach the vast information on the World Wide Web. Recent studies indicatethat Web searching, behind email, is the second most popular activities on the Internet. Surveys indicate that there are hundreds of thousands of search engines on the Web. Not only Web users interact with search engines, many Web applicationsalso need to interact with search engines. For example,metasearch engines utilize existing search engines to performsearch [22] and need to extract the search results from the resultpages returned by the search engines used. As another example,deep web crawling is to crawl documents or data records from(deep web) search engines [24] and it too needs to extract thesearch results from the result pages returned by search engines.

2. Background Information

2.1.Web Search Engines

In this work, both the traditional crawler-based"Surface Web" search engines and "Deep Web" databasesthat have Web search interfaces are regarded as Websearch engines. Please refer to [2] to for detaileddiscussion of Surface Web and Deep Web. Also, in [10]and [13], we described in detail issues that arise due to thelargeness of the number of search engines that we areaiming to metasearch.We call a webpage from which users can type inqueries a *search engine interface*, or a *search engine page*.

2.2.Search Engine Form

On the *search engine interface*, there is at least one*HTML form*, allowing users to submit queries. To identifysuch forms is of crucial importance in discovery. Pleaserefer to [12] to learn more about HTML forms.

2.3. Search Engine Result Page

After a query is sent to a search engine, a *result page* isreturned. Usually, retrieved documents are listed on thepage, with their descriptions and URLs. Some otherimportant information about the search (such as the numberof retrieved documents for a query) may be present. A metasearch engine needs to extract result document URLsand other information from result pages returned from allmetasearched search engines to formulate its own resultpages to return to metasearch engine users.

2.4. Automatic Search Engine Discovery

We propose a two-step process (crawling and filtering)to discover search engines.

Step 1. Crawling. A special Web crawler is created tofetch webpages. Each webpage is regarded as a potentialsearch engine interface page.

Step 2. Filtering. A set of recognition rules is thenapplied to determine if the page has a search engineinterface. The following are the main filtering rules in thecurrent implementation:

(1) The HTML source file of a search engineinterface page should contain at least one HTMLform.

(2) The form must also have a *text input control* forquery input.

(3) At least one of a set of keywords such as "search,""query" or "find" appears either in the form tag orin the text immediately preceding or following the"<form>" tag.

2.5. Automatic Search Engine Connection

Automatic search engine connection involves four steps.

1. Parse HTML source code of a candidate webpageinto a tree structure of HTML tags. For the sake ofillustration, Figure 1 is a tree structurepresentation for the following simple HTML page:

```
<html>
<head>
<title>example</title>
</head>
<body>
<form>...</form>
</body>
</html>
```

Figure 1

2. Extract form parameters and attributes from theFORM sub-tree and save them into an XMLformatted file, which we call the *search enginedescription file* of the search engine.

3. Read the form information from the

search enginedescription file and re-construct a test querystring.

4. Send the test query to check connection correctness. If some http error code is returned,showing connection failure, further manualanalysis may be needed to handle the exception.

2.6. Search Engine Result Extraction

The two pieces of information extracted from thereturned page are: (1) The URLs and/or snippets ofretrieved webpages. (2) The total number of retrieveddocuments, as described in Section 2.

There are two steps in automatic result extraction.

Step 1. A so-called *"impossible query"* (a queryconsisting of a non-existent term) is sent. All URLs on theresult page are useless in terms of document retrieval. Theyare recorded and easily excluded from result pages forother queries. The layout pattern of the "Result Not Found"page is also recorded for future reference.

Step 2. A number of program-generated queries are sent.The result pages are compared against each other and allthe common URLs are marked as useless. Two tasks areyet to be undertaken:

1. Find the URLs of returned result documents:

The patterns of result document URLs on the same resultpage are very similar. We use a unique feature, called *"TagPrefix,"* to represent the layout pattern.The *Tag Prefix* of a URL is a sequence of HTML tagsthat appear before a URL and typically on the same line asthe URL.For example, a section of HTML code may look likethis:

<table><tr><td><b><a
href=http://url1.html>url1
Caption</a></b></td></tr> ... </table>

The tag prefix of the URL http://url1.html is "<tr><td><b>" since the tag "<tr>" implies change of aline. Other tags indicating such a change include "<p>","<br>", "<table>", "<hr>", "<LI>", and so on.

2 Find the number of matched documents

This information usually appears either at thebeginning or at the bottom of a result page on a text line,which may be set apart by some specific features, such asthe presence of numeric numbers, or special keywords(e.g. *found, returned, matches, results*, etc.), or the *"of"* pattern (e.g. 1-20 *of* 200), or the query terms. We call thisline *"document hits line"*. It needs to be automaticallyextracted.

SYSTEM ARCHITECTURE

Figure 1 shows the architecture of our automatic wrappergeneration system. The input to the system is the URL of a searchengine's interface page, which contains an HTML *form* used toaccept user queries. The output of the system is a *wrapper* for thesearch engine. The *search engine form extractor* figures out howto connect to the search engine using the information available inthe HTML *form*. Based on the extracted form information, the*query sender* component sends queries to the search engine andreceives result pages returned by the search engine. Readers mayrefer to [28] for more details about these two components.

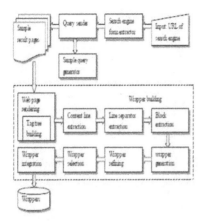

Figure 1. System Architecture of ViNTs

The *wrapper-building module*, shown in the dash-line box above,is the focus of this paper. The input to this module is a set ofsample result pages produced by a search engine in response toautomatically generated sample queries. The only requirement fora sample result page is that it contains a sufficient number ofSRRs (at least four, and the more the better), to permit theregularities among the SRRs to be explored for wrapper building.The input to this module also contains a special result page calledno-result page, which contains no SRRs. This page contains onlyinformation irrelevant to any user query and thus can be used tofilter out useless information from other result pages. The samplequery that yields the *no-result page* is called an *impossible query*.All sample queries are generated by the *sample query generator*.This component has been implemented in our system but it willnot be discussed in this paper.To utilize the visual content features, we render each sampleresult page during wrapper building. There are many objects suchas *links* and

texts on each result page (*Anchor text* associated witha URL is called a link in this paper). When a result page isrendered, for each object on the result page, a *rendering box* – arectangle containing the object – is produced. We use a coordinatesystem based on the browser window to help describe thepositions of the rendering boxes. Our wrapper generation methodis sketched below. First, for each sample result page, we analyzethe types (say link or text) and the positions of all the renderingboxes to identify some candidate result records (section 4). Basedon these records and a hypothesis about the general format of theSRR wrappers, we build some initial wrappers. These wrappers are refined to enable the detection of theboundaries separating different types of records (e.g., SRRs andnon-SRRs) (section 5.5). Next, the most promising wrapper isselected for this result page from the refined wrappers usingadditional visual features (section 5.6). Some search engines mayproduce different irrelevant information on different result pages(e.g., the advertisements may be query dependent). As a result,different sample result pages may lead to slightly differentwrappers. Our final step is to integrate the wrappers for all sampleresult pages of the search engine to produce the final wrapper forthe search engine (section 5.7). The detail of our method will bepresented in the next several sections.

3. Proposed system

As mentioned earlier, existing techniques on web informationextraction are based on the analysis of HTML tag structures. Webelieve that regularities in visual content (strings, images, etc. asshown on web pages) should also be utilized to achieve higherperformance.Many visual content features that are designed to help peoplelocate and understand information on a web page can helpinformation extraction. For example, the profile (or contour) ofthe left side of each SRR on the same result page tends to be verysimilar to each other, there are visual separators (e.g., blank lines)between consecutive SRRs, all SRRs tend to be arranged togetherin a special section on the result page, and this section occupies alarge portion on the result page, and it also tends to be centrallylocated on the page. We describe some basic visual contentfeatures that are used in this study in the following sub-sections.

3.1 Content Line

A result page usually consists of multiple sections, eachcontaining information in one category. For example, the resultpage in Figure 2 consists of two sections: the one on the leftcontains SRRs and the one on the right contains sponsored links.The section containing SRRs will be called the *SRR section*.

Definition 3.1 (Content line) *A content line is a group ofcharacters that visually form a horizontal line in the same sectionon the rendered page.*In Figure 2, "Category: Home > Personal Finance > TaxPreparation" forms a content line. Note that "Tax Info Center"forms a different content line even though it is visually in thesame line as the line starting with "Category:" because theyappear in different sections on the result page.

Figure 2. A result page by Google

Different types of content lines can be observed on typical resultpages and their arrangements are useful for identifying records. Inour approach, the following types of content lines are identified:

- LINK – more than 90% of the area of the rendering box ofthis line is link area. Only anchor text (i.e., clickable text)with an underlying URL is considered a link in this paper.Thus, a URL that is not an anchor text is not considered as alink, but as a text. [code: 1]
- TEXT – more than 90% of the area of the rendering box ofthis line is text area. [code: 2]
- LINK-TEXT – it contains both link and text, none of themoccupies more than 90% of the area. [code 3]
- LINK-HEAD – link line but started with a number like 1, 2,3, ... [code: 4]
- TEXT-HEAD – text line but started with a number. [code: 5]
- LINK-TEXT-HEAD – link-text line but started with anumber. [code: 6]
- HR-LINE – a visual line generated by HTML tag <HR>.[code: 7]
- BLANK – the blank line. [code: 8]

The record in Figure 3 contains 5 content lines. The first is aLINK line, followed by two TEXT lines, then another LINK lineand the last (invisible) is a BLANK line. To facilitatecomputation, a *code* is assigned to each type of content line.Each content line has a rendering box and the left x coordinate ofthe rendering box is called the *position code* of the content line.The position code of a blank line is set to be the position code ofthe visible line immediately before it. To summarize, each contentline is represented as a (type code, position code) pair.

3.2 Shape of a Block

A record consists of one or more content lines, which togetherform a *block*. An observation about the records on a result page isthat the left side profiles of all records in the same section tend tobe very similar, and records from different sections tend to havedifferent left side profiles. This observation is consistent with thefact that result pages are generated by computer programs anddifferent sections are usually generated by different scripts. Wedefine block shape to represent the left side profile of a block.

Definition 3.2 (Shape of a block) *Let $c1$, ..., ck be the content lines in a block in top-down order and let pci be the position code of $ci, i=1,...,k$. The shape of the block is an ordered list of the position codes of the member content lines of the block, namely $(pc1, ...,pck)$. $(pc1, ..., pck)$ is also called the shape code of the block.*

Consider the block in Figure 3. It has 5 content lines (the fifth is a blank line). Suppose the position codes of the 5 content lines from top to bottom are 8, 48, 48, 48 and 48, respectively. Then the shape of the block is represented as (8, 48, 48, 48, 48).

3.3 Block Similarity

Each block consists of three pieces of information: the ordered (from top to bottom) type codes of its content lines, the position codes of Its content lines and the block shape. We define three

metrics to measure the similarity between two blocks of content lines: *type distance, shape distance* and *position distance*.

Type distance. The type distance between two blocks is to capture the difference in their content line type sequences. The detail is described below. We define the *type code of a block* as a sequence of the type codes of the content lines of the block. Let TCi be the type code of the ith content line in the block, then $TC1...TCn$ is the type code of the block, where n is the number of content lines in the block. Furthermore, multiple consecutive TEXT type codes are compressed to one occurrence based on the observation that texts in snippets of SRRs often vary in lengths significantly. Based on the above definition, the type code for the block .

In our implementation, type distance between two blocks a and b is the *edit distance* [27] between the type codes of the

two blocks. **Shape distance**. This distance is to measure difference between the indention sequences of the shapes of two blocks. To focus on the shape and ignore where a block starts in the coordinate system, we subtract the smallest position code in a shape code from each position code. This will convert (8, 48, 48, 48, 48) to (0, 40, 40, 40, 40). To concentrate on indentions, multiple consecutive occurrences of the same position code are suppressed to one. Consequently, (0, 40, 40, 40, 40) is transformed to (0, 40), indicating that the shape has one indention with indent value 40. The final list will be called the *modified shape code* of a block. Let $MSC(u)$ denote the modified shape code of block u. For the

block shapes in Figure 4, if we assume the value of each indent is 10, then we have $MSC(a)$ = (0), $MSC(b)$ = (0, 10), $MSC(c)$ = (0,10), $MSC(d)$ = (0, 10, 20), $MSC(e)$ = (10, 0) and $MSC(f)$ = (0, 10,0). Note that blocks b and c have the same modified shape code while other blocks all have different modified shape codes. In summary, the shape of a block is represented as a sequence of indentions in our method. The shape distance of two blocks a and b is defined as the maximum difference between the corresponding modified shape codes of the two blocks; if one modified shape code is longer than the other, we pad the shorter one with 0's at the end to make the lengths of the two shape codes the same before calculating their shape distance.

Position distance. This distance measures the difference between the closest points of the two blocks to the left boundary of the rendered result page. In other words, the position distance
a b c d e f between two blocks a and b is the difference between the smallest position code for any content line in a and that in b.

3.4 Wrapper Format Hypothesis

A wrapper defined over a tag tree needs to specify two things: (a)the location of the minimal sub-tree t that contains all SRRs, and(b) the separator set. The minimal sub-tree of t can be determinedby a tag path from the root of the tag tree to the root of t. Within t,SRRs are separated by possibly different kinds of separators andeach separator is also (the ending) part of a record. In addition, asearch engine may display only certain number of SRRs on aresult page. Based on the above analysis, we hypothesize that awrapper can be represented as the following regular expression:prefix (X (separator1 | separator2 | ...))[min, max] (1)where X is a wild card for sub-forests of the tag tree, *prefix* is a tagpath, separators are also sub-forests of the tag tree, "|" is thealternation operator, the concatenation of X and a separatorcorresponds to a record, min and max are used to select recordsfrom a list of records. For example, if the wrapper without the[min, max] restriction extracts a list of n records, then only therecords between the min-th and the max-th records are extracted.In general, min ≥ 0 and max can be infinite (some search enginesdo not limit the number of results that can be displayed on a resultpage). The *prefix* determines the minimal sub-tree t that containsall SRRs in the result page. The *separators* are used to segment alldescendants of t into SRRs.Once such a wrapper is generated for a search engine, extractingSRRs from a result page of the search engine is straightforward.First we parse the result page and build the tag tree. Next, wefollow the *prefix* of the wrapper to locate the root of the minimalsub-tree t that contains all SRRs. Then we find all existingoccurrences of the separators in the descendants of t, and arrangethem in the

order of their appearances in the sub-tree t. We extractthe ith SRR from the descendant nodes of t located within the $i$thand ($i+1$)th occurrences of separators (the nodes representing the($i+1$)th occurrence of separators are part of the ith SRR). Finally,we extract the SRRs whose serial numbers are within the range[min, max].

3.5 Initial Wrapper Building

For a give candidate record group, we form sub-groups ofconsecutive records of size k ($k = 3$ is used in our experiment).The first k records form one sub-group, the second to the ($k+1$)th records form the next sub-group, and so on. With the tag paths ofthe records in each sub-group and the hypothesis about the formatof the wrapper (expression (1)), we try to build an initial wrapperfor the records in each sub-group. It is possible that differentinitial wrappers will be generated for different sub-groups. It isalso possible that no initial wrapper can be generated for somesub-groups. All produced wrappers will be passed to therefinement step of our method.We now discuss how to generate an initial wrapper for a subgroupG. In this step, we focus on identifying the *prefix* and the*separator(s)* in expression (1). Parameters *min* and *max* will bedetermined later in a refinement step (section 5.5). Suppose therecords in G appear in order r1, ..., rk. Let path(ri) denote the tagpath of ri. The tag paths for the second, third and fourth records in will be used as a running example to explain our method.

The main ideas of our method are as follows.

1. We find the maximum common prefix PRE of all input tagpaths (i.e., those for records in G). For our running example,we have PRE = <HTML>C<HEAD>S <BODY> C<IMG> S<CENTER>S<HR>S<B>S<HR>S<DL>S. Note

that thisPRE may be different from the *prefix* needed by expression(1). The reason is that the first record of the group (the onewith the shortest tag path) may not be in G. In general, thecorrect prefix is contained in PRE but PRE may contain extrapath nodes at the end. To identify the extra path nodes, wefirst remove PRE from each tag path (let p_i = path(r_i) − PRE)and then compute Diff$_i$ = p_{i+1} − p_i (p_i is a suffix of p_{i+1}). If all Diff's are the same, then it is a *separator* for expression (1).In our running example, Diff = <DL>S is the separator. Wenow remove all occurrences of Diff from the end of PRE. LetPRE1 be the new PRE and E be the last node of PRE1. Atthis point, an effort is made to identify additional separatorsbased on whether the tag path of Diff is identical to the tagpattern composed of the child node(s) of E and whether Diffalso appears immediately before E. When both conditions aresatisfied, the path node of E is identified as a new separatorand the occurrences of all separators (including previouslyidentified ones) are removed from the end of PRE1. Thisprocess is repeated until no new separator can be identifiedand the remaining tag path (of PRE1) is the prefix forexpression (1). For our running example, only one separatoris identified and the correct prefix is <HTML> C <HEAD> S<BODY> C <IMG> S <CENTER> S<HR>S <B>S<HR>S.2. If Diffs are different, three cases are identified. Case 1: Acommon suffix of the Diffs does not exist. In this case, thewrapper generating process fails and the process isterminated. Case 2: A common suffix exists and it does nothave multiple occurrences in any Diff. In this case, this suffixis a *separator*. We subtract from PRE any suffix that isidentical to any of the Diffs until no further subtraction ispossible and the remaining PRE is the *prefix* for expression(1). Case 3: All common suffixes have multiple occurrencesin some Diffs. In this case, an attempt is made to expandeach Diff by taking the structure of the child nodes (or evendeeper descendant nodes) of the nodes in the Diff intoconsideration (structures of child nodes help differentiatedifferent nodes in the Diff and therefore help to find aseparator that does not have multiple occurrences in Diffs).The expanded Diffs are then used to identify separators as inthe second case. If the separator still cannot be found, thewrapper building process fails.

3. Based on the *prefix* and *separator(s)* identified in the last twosteps, an initial wrapper is generated for G by assuming *min*= 0 and *max* = ∞. For example, the initial wrapper generated for the running example is <HTML>C<HEAD>S<BODY>C<IMG>S<CENTER>S<HR>S<B>S<HR>S(X<DL>S)[0, ∞],where X is a wild card. The initial wrapper is then used toextract all matching records from the result page to see if allrecords in G can be correctly extracted in consecutive order.If this is true, the wrapper is accepted for further evaluation(refinement in section 5.5). If this is not true, a possiblereason is that the separator used is incorrect. Therefore, anattempt is made to expand the nodes in the separator by their child (descendant) nodes as in Step 2 to see if a newseparator can be found. If it can be found, it is used to revisethe initial wrapper and repeat the above process. If the newwrapper cannot be accepted or a new separator cannot befound, the wrapper building process fails for G.

3.6 Wrapper Refining

This task is to determine the values of the parameters *min* and *max*of a wrapper (see expression (1)). The input to the wrapperrefining process includes an initial wrapper (generated in section5.4) and a list of consecutive records extracted by applying thewrapper. Let these records be numbered from 1 to n, and let Rmbe the record in the middle. The wrapper refining process worksas follows. We start from Rm and move towards the two ends ofthe list. Let's consider the process of moving towards thebeginning of the list. When the next record is encountered, if itdoes not contain a link or its block is not visually similar to the

block of Rm, the serial number of the record plus 1 becomes min.similarly, max can be determined when we consider the processof moving towards the end of the list.

3.7 Wrapper Selection for One Sample Page

At this step, we have a set of wrappers and record groupsextracted by applying those wrappers. Among these wrappers,four cases may occur. First, some wrappers can correctly extractall SRRs and nothing else. Second, some may extract some butnot all correct SRRs. Third, some may retrieval all SRRs but alsosome non-SRR records. Fourth, some may be suitable for otherneatly arranged information on the result page such as ads andhost information. The wrapper selection step is to determine thewrapper that mostly likely belongs to the first case.Our approach uses content features (both visual and non-visual) tohelp find the correct SRR group hence the correct wrapper. It isnot difficult to observe that on the rendered result page, the correct SRR group likely (1) occupies a large area, (2) is centrallylocated, (3) contains many characters, (4) has a large number ofrecords. To utilize these content features, we define the followingfour weights:

1. *Rendering area weight* (RAW). A group's RAW is definedas the relative rendering area of this record group over thelargest rendering area of all record groups.

2. *Center distance weight* (CDW). CDW is based on thedistance between the center of a group's rendering box andthe center of the rendering box of the whole result page; thisdistance is called the *center distance* of the group. Let p0 bethe center of the whole page's rendering box. If the renderingbox of a group contains p0, its center distance is defined to be0; otherwise we use the Euclid distance between the center ofthe group's rendering box and p0. We define CDW as therelative center distance over the smallest center distance.

3. *Number of records weight* (NRW). A group's NRW isdefined as the number of records of the group divided by thenumber of records of the largest group.

4. *Average number of characters weight* (ACNW). The averagenumber of characters of a group is the average number ofcharacters in each block in this group. A group's ACNW isdefined as the relative average number of characters of thegroup over the largest average number of characters in allgroups.

We combine the above four weights by weighted summation, pickthe group with the highest combined weight as the search resultgroup and output its corresponding wrapper as the correct wrapperfor the input sample page.

3.8 Wrapper Integration

After wrapper selection, we are able to build a wrapper for eachsample result page. The wrappers built from different sampleresult pages of the same search engine may be different eventhough they are all correct with respect to their correspondingsample result pages. The reason is that frequently search enginesmay include information on a result page that is query dependentor changes from time to time. As a result, the tag paths (*prefixes*in wrapper expressions) of the minimal sub-tree that contains allSRRs as well as the separator sets may vary. Thus, a wrapper builtfrom one sample page may not correctly extract SRRs whenapplied to another page. Wrapper integration is to integrate thewrappers built from multiple sample result pages of the samesearch engine into a single robust wrapper for the search engine.

The integration involves three parts: separator integration, prefixintegration and [min, max] integration. During the integrationprocess, two wrappers are considered at a time. If both their separator sets and their prefixes can be integrated, the twowrappers are integrated. An integrated wrapper may then beintegrated with another (possibly integrated) wrapper. At the endof this process, there may be multiple integrated wrappers and nointegration between them can be carried out. At this time, theintegrated wrapper with the largest support (i.e., it is integratedfrom the largest number of input wrappers) will be selected as thefinal wrapper for the search engine. In our currentimplementation, tie is broken arbitrarily. In the following, we outline how two wrappers are integrated.

Separator integration:
For two separator sets, if one set is a subset of the other set, wetake the larger set as the integrated separator set. The case that thetwo separator sets are identical is a special case of the above case.If none of the sets is a subset of the other, the integration of thesetwo separator sets fails.

Prefix integration:
Prefix integration is carried out by converting each prefix into a*compact form* through the removal of unimportant path nodes.This would remove "noises" from the prefixes.The conversion is based on the

following rules:
(1) Keep all path nodes with direction code of "C".
(2) Keep path nodes with direction code of "S" only if their tagname is the same as that of the closest future path node withdirection code of "C".
(3) For any path node after the last node with direction code "C",if its tag name is identical to the tag name of the first node ofany separator in the wrapper, it is kept; otherwise it isdeleted.

For example, the prefix of the wrapper becomes <HTML>C<BODY>C. It is obvious that the compactprefix will find the same minimal sub-tree as the original *prefix.*Prefix integration can be carried out reasonably easily afterprefixes are converted into compact forms.

[min, max] integration:
Let the two input [min, max]'s be [min1, max1] and [min2,max2], respectively. Let [min3, max3] be the integration result.Then min3 = min {min1, min2} and max3 = max {max1, max2}.

4 VISUAL BLOCK TREE AND VISUAL FEATURES

Before the main techniques of our approach are presented,we describe the basic concepts and visual features that ourapproach needs.

4.1 Visual Information of Web Pages

The information on Web pages consists of both texts andimages (static pictures, flash, video, etc.). The visualinformation of Web pages used in this paper includesmostly information related to Web page layout (location andsize) and font.

4.1.1 Web Page Layout

A coordinate system can be built for every Web page. Theorigin locates at the top left corner of the Web page. TheX-axis is horizontal left-right, and the Y-axis is vertical topdown.Suppose each text/image is contained in a minimumbounding rectangle with sides parallel to the axes. Then, atext/image can have an exact coordinate (x, y) on the Webpage. Here, x refers to the horizontal distance between theorigin and the left side of its corresponding rectangle, while

y refers to the vertical distance between the origin and theupper side of its corresponding box. The size of a text/image is its height and width.The coordinates and sizes of texts/images on the Webpage make up the Web page layout.

4.1.2 Font

The fonts of the texts on a Web page are also very usefulvisual information, which are determined by many attributesas shown in Table 1. Two fonts are considered to be thesame only if they have the same value under each attribute.

4.2 Deep Web Page Representation

The visual information of Web pages, which has beenintroduced above, can be obtained through the programminginterface provided by Web browsers (i.e., IE). In thispaper, we employ the VIPS algorithm [4] to transform a deepWeb page into a Visual Block tree and extract the visualinformation.AVisual Block tree is actually a segmentation ofa Web page. The root block represents the whole page,

Font Attributes and Examplesthe Web page. The leaf blocks are the blocks that cannot besegmented further, and they represent the minimumsemantic units, such as continuous texts or images. Fig. 2ashows a popular presentation structure of deep Web pagesand Fig. 2b gives its corresponding Visual Block tree. Thetechnical details of building Visual Block

andeach block in the tree corresponds to a rectangular region on

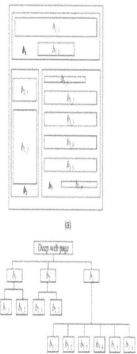

Fig. 2. (a) The presentation structure and (b) its Visual Block tree.

trees can be foundin [4]. An actual Visual Block tree of a deep Web page maycontain hundreds even thousands of blocks.

CONCLUSIONS AND FUTURE WORKS

Our approach consists of four primary steps: VisualBlock tree building, data record extraction, data itemextraction, and visual wrapper generation. Visual Blocktree building is to build the Visual Block tree for a givensample deep page using the VIPS algorithm. With theVisual Block tree, data record extraction and data itemextraction are carried out based on our proposed visualfeatures. Visual wrapper generation is to generate thewrappers that can improve the efficiency of both datarecord extraction and data item extraction. Highly accurateexperimental results provide strong evidence that richvisual features on deep Web pages can be used as the basisto design highly effective data extraction algorithms.However, there are still some remaining issues and weplan to address them in the future. First, we can onlyprocess deep Web pages containing one data region, whilethere is significant number of multidata-region deep Web pages. Though Zhao et al. [21] have attempted to addressthis problem, their solution is HTML-dependent and itsperformance has a large room for improvement. We intendto propose a vision-based approach to tackle this problem.Second, the efficiency of system can be improved. In thecurrent system, the visual information of Web pages isobtained by calling the programming APIs of IE, which is atime-consuming process. To address this problem, weintend to develop a set of new APIs to obtain the visualinformation directly from the Web pages.

REFERENCES

[1] B. Adelberg. NoDoSE – A tool for semi-automatically
extracting structured and semistructured data from text
documents. ACM SIGMOD Conference, 1998.
[2] A. Arasu, H. Garcia-Molina. Extracting Structured Data from
Web Pages. ACM SIGMOD Conference, June 2003.
[3] R. Baumgartner, S. Flesca and G. Gottlob. Visual web
information extraction with Lixto. VLDB Conference, 2001.
[4] M. Bergman. The Deep Web: Surfacing Hidden Value.
White Paper, BrightPlanet, 2000 (www.completeplanet.com/ Tutorials/DeepWeb/index.asp)
[5] D. Buttler, L. Liu, C. Pu. A Fully Automated Object
Extraction System for the World Wide Web. International
Conference on Distributed Computing Systems (ICDCS 2001), 2001.
[6] C. Chang, S. Lui. IEPAD: Information Extraction based on
Pattern Discovery. World Wide Web Conference, 2001.
[7] K. Chang, B. He, C. Li, M. P, Z. Zhang. Structured
Databases on the Web: Observations and Implications.
Technical Report, UIUCDCS-R-2003-2321, UIUC, 2003.
[8] L. Chen, H. Jamil, N. Wang. Automatic Composite Wrapper
Generation for Semi-Structured Biological Data Based on
Table Structure Identification. SIGMOD Record, June 2004.
[9] D.W. Embley, Y.S. Jiang, and Y.-K. Ng, "Record-Boundary
Discovery in Web Documents," Proc. ACM SIGMOD, pp. 467-478, 1999.
[10] W. Gatterbauer, P. Bohunsky, M. Herzog, B. Krpl, and B. Pollak,
"Towards Domain Independent Information Extraction from Web
Tables," Proc. Int'l World Wide Web Conf. (WWW), pp. 71-80, 2007.

[11] J. Hammer, J. McHugh, and H. Garcia-Molina, "Semistructured Data: The TSIMMIS Experience," Proc. East-European Workshop Advances in Databases and Information Systems (ADBIS), pp. 1-8, 1997.
[12] C.-N. Hsu and M.-T. Dung, "Generating Finite-State Transducers for Semi-Structured Data Extraction from the Web," Information Systems, vol. 23, no. 8, pp. 521-538, 1998.
[13] http://daisen.cc.kyushu-u.ac.jp/TBDW/, 2009.
[14] http://www.w3.org/html/wg/html5/, 2009.
[15] N. Kushmerick, "Wrapper Induction: Efficiency and Expressiveness," Artificial Intelligence, vol. 118, nos. 1/2, pp. 15-68, 2000.
[16] A. Laender, B. Ribeiro-Neto, A. da Silva, and J. Teixeira, "A Brief Survey of Web Data Extraction Tools," SIGMOD Record, vol. 31, no. 2, pp. 84-93, 2002.
[17] B. Liu, R.L. Grossman, and Y. Zhai, "Mining Data Records in Web Pages," Proc. Int'l Conf. Knowledge Discovery and Data Mining (KDD), pp. 601-606, 2003.
[18] W. Liu, X. Meng, and W. Meng, "Vision-Based Web Data Records Extraction," Proc. Int'l Workshop Web and Databases (WebDB '06), pp. 20-25, June 2006.
[19] L. Liu, C. Pu, and W. Han, "XWRAP: An XML-Enabled Wrapper Construction System for Web Information Sources," Proc. Int'l Conf. Data Eng. (ICDE), pp. 611-621, 2000.
[20] Y. Lu, H. He, H. Zhao, W. Meng, and C.T. Yu, "Annotating Structured Data of the Deep Web," Proc. Int'l Conf. Data Eng. (ICDE), pp. 376-385, 2007.
[21] J. Madhavan, S.R. Jeffery, S. Cohen, X.L. Dong, D. Ko, C. Yu, and A. Halevy, "Web-Scale Data Integration: You Can Only Afford to Pay As You Go," Proc. Conf. Innovative Data Systems Research (CIDR), pp. 342-350, 2007.